S0-DFH-913

Quick & Healthy
Daily juicepresso

Published in 2013 by Coway Co., Ltd

16F, Joongang Ilbo BLDG., 88, Seosomun-ro, Jung-gu, Seoul,
100-759, Korea
www.coway.com

Copyright © 2013 Coway Co., Ltd.

All rights reserved. No part of this publication may be reproduced, stored or transmitted in any form or by any means, electronic, mechanical, photocopying, recording or otherwise, without the prior written consent of the publisher, Coway Co., Ltd.

Notice

As a safety precaution, please read all enclosed material thoroughly prior to using your Juicepresso. This book
is not designed to and does not provide medical advice, professional diagnosis, opinions or treatment and should not be used as a substitute for medical or professional care. No responsibility is assumed by the publisher and authors for any errors or omissions that may be found in the text. We accept no liability for any injuries or damages that may occur as a result of any reliance on the information contained in the text.

**For more information on Juicepresso,
visit our website at www.juicepressousa.com**

ISBN 979-11-8507-708-6

Printed and bound in the Republic of South Korea

First English language edition

Planning & production : Coway Co., Ltd.
Book design & recipe development : Achefcompany Co., Ltd

Quick & Healthy

Daily **juice**presso

Smart Extraction System

Prologue

Squeeze nature, Taste Juicepresso

juícepresso's 3 in 1 Smart Extraction System does not grind but presses ingredients for the highest extraction rate, highest nutritional content and juice that does not separate.

Simple to use. Easy to clean.

Contents

Part.1 About *juice*presso

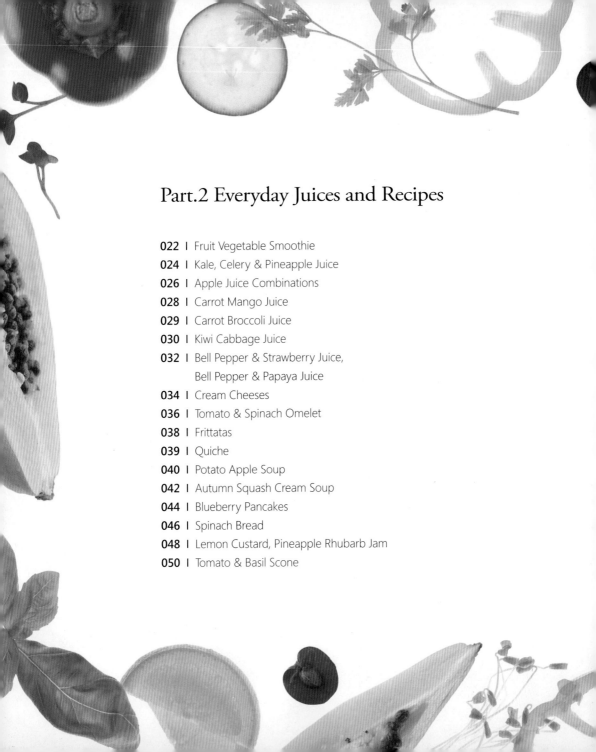

Part.2 Everyday Juices and Recipes

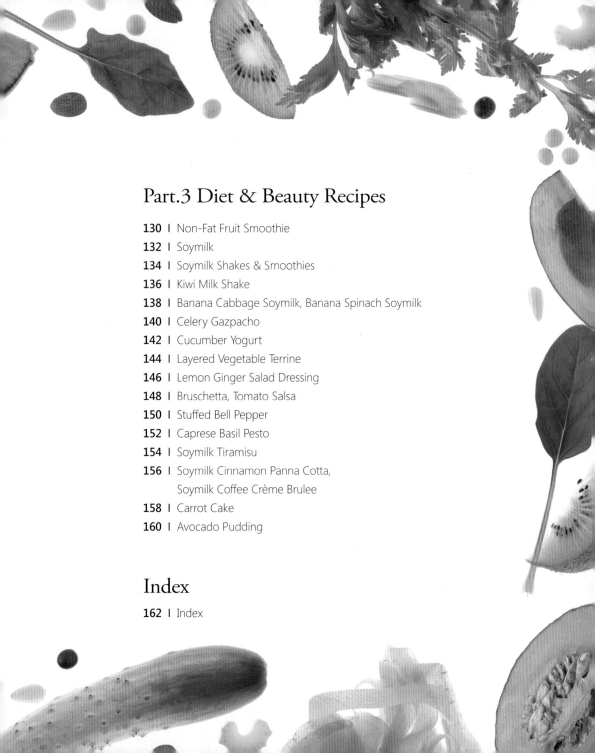

Part.3 Diet & Beauty Recipes

Index

Part.1
About **juice**presso

Smart Extraction System

The Benefits of **juíce**presso

QUICK   Press nutrient rich vegetable and fruit juices in minutes.

EASY   Simple assembly & quick clean up.

HEALTHY   The most efficient way to increase your intake of vitamins, minerals, enzymes, fiber, and give your energy levels a boost.

SMART   **juíce**presso produces a much dryer pulp.
This means the highest possible amount of juice is extracted leaving less waste and giving you significant savings.

VARIETY   **juíce**presso extracts only the undiluted juice of ingredients. Color, texture and consistency never waiver regardless of what you juice.

Assembly Instructions

1. Attach the drum to the main body. The drum should be fully inserted into the shaft of the main body.

2. Place the squeezing screw into the center of the drum. Push down, into place.

Drum

Squeezing Screw

3. Place the hopper onto the drum and turn it clockwise. Ensure that the "Open" dot(●) on the hopper is aligned with the "dot"(●) on the body.

How to use Your **juíce**presso

1. Place your **juíce**presso on a solid, flat surface.

2. Cut ingredients into pieces that will easily fit into the feeding shoot.

3. Put pitchers under the pulp and juice outlet prior to inserting ingredients.

4. Begin feeding ingredients into the machine.

5. Turn the power "On".

6. Continue feeding ingredients into the machine until you have the desired quantity of juice.
(Warning! Do not operate machine longer than 20 minutes at a time.)

How to Disassemble and Clean

1. Turn machine "off" and unplug from the electrical outlet.
2. Hold and twist the hopper to unlock. Make sure "dot" is aligned with the "open" sign before removing.
3. Disassembly order – Hopper, Squeezing Screw, Drum.
4. Use the brush to thoroughly clean the squeezing screw. Rinse under cool water to remove any additional matter.
5. Wash and rinse the hopper, drum and cleaning brush in cool water.
6. Dry all part with a clean soft cloth.

The squeezing screw, drum and pitchers are all dishwasher safe. Simply rinse and place in the dishwasher!

Cleaning Tip! Clean juicer immediately after use.

DO NOT RINSE OR SUBMERGE THE MAIN BODY IN WATER OR ANY OTHER LIQUID. The main body can be cleaned with a clean, soft cloth.

How to Store Juice and Reuse Pulp

JUICE: The fresh fruits and vegetables are pressed extracting the nectar directly from the pulp. That pressing action, instead of blending or grinding, won't oxidize or degrade the fruit and vegetables and helps keep the nutrients and enzymes intact. Because of this process, pressed juices will keep in the refrigerator, in an airtight container, for up to 2 days.

PULP: Fresh pulp should be stored in an airtight container and refrigerated. For best results, use them within two days. You may also freeze the pulp indefinitely in an airtight container.

Nutrition information

Bananas

Sports enthusiasts appreciate the potassium-power delivered by this high-energy fruit. Bananas may help to prevent high blood pressure and protect against atherosclerosis. They have long been recognized for their anti-acid effects that protect against stomach ulcers and ulcer damage.

Apples

Apples are high in soluble fiber and have a high water content, which makes them great for constipation and digestive issues. The peel is high in antioxidants and the phytonutrients found in apples help regulate blood sugar.

Blueberries

Blueberries have one of the highest antioxidant capacities of any fruit or vegetable there is. They have a low glycemic index, which is great for people with diabetes and studies show blueberries can improve memory. They are also a very good source of Vitamin C, Vitamin K and Manganese.

Lemons

Low in calories, zero fat or cholesterol, lemons are rich in dietary fiber. An excellent source of vitamin C, one lemon provides 88% of the daily-recommended intake. Vitamin C also helps the human body develop resistance against infectious agents and harmful, pro-inflammatory free radicals in the blood.

Spinach

Among the World's Healthiest vegetables, spinach is at the top of the list for nutrient richness. High in vitamins and minerals, it is also concentrated in health-promoting phytonutrients such as carotenoids (beta-carotene, lutein, and zeaxanthin) and flavonoids to provide you with powerful antioxidant protection. Spinach may also help protect against inflammatory problems, oxidative stress-related problems, cardiovascular problems, bone problems, and cancers.

Tomatoes

Tomatoes are widely known for their outstanding antioxidant content, including, of course, their rich concentration of lycopene. Researchers have recently found an important connection between lycopene, its antioxidant properties, and bone health. Fresh tomatoes have also been shown to help lower total cholesterol, LDL cholesterol, and triglycerides.

Carrots

Carrots are perhaps best known for their rich supply of the antioxidant nutrient beta-carotene. Abundant and grown throughout the year, they also offer a wide variety of antioxidants and other health-supporting nutrients. Studies have shown carrots protect against cardiovascular disease and offer many anti-cancer benefits.

Bell Peppers

Bell peppers are a very good source of vitamin E at about 1.45 milligrams per cup, and they contain more than 30 different carotenoids, including excellent amounts of beta-carotene and zeaxanthin. Both of these carotenoids provide antioxidant and anti-inflammatory health benefits. They are also excellent source of vitamin C at 117 milligrams per cup. That's more than twice the amount of vitamin C found in a typical orange.

Part. 2
Everyday Juices and Recipes

A fresh pressed juice is an excellent way to start your morning. Juices help gently detox the body of free radicals and boost your energy so you are ready to face your day.

Fruit & Vegetable Smoothie

★ ★ ✦

A delicious way to get your daily requirement of fruits and veggies.

Ingredients: Makes 2 Servings

½ mango
2 oz spinach
¼ cup milk
½ cup yogurt
20 grapes
½ apple
1 carrot
1 banana
1½ tbsp. agave syrup

Directions

1. Peel mango, cut in half (removing the center seed).

2. Mix milk with yogurt.

3. Squeeze in order—Mango, grapes, apple, carrot, banana, spinach.

4. Add pressed juice to milk and yogurt and stir in agave.

Kale Celery Pineapple Juice

Packed with fiber and nutrients, kale and celery make this delicious juice an antioxidant winner.

Ingredients: Makes 2 Servings

1½ oz. kale
½ cup celery
1¾ cup chopped pineapple (Canned or fresh may be used.)
1½ tbsp. agave syrup

Directions

1. Rinse and chop celery and kale.

2. Peel and cut pineapple and kiwi into suitable sized pieces. Add syrup into the blend and stir.

3. Press in order—Kale, celery, pineapple.

4. Stir in agave syrup and serve.

Tip

Add more agave to lessen bitterness.

Apple Kiwi
Juice

Apple Grapefruit
Juice

Apple Pear
Juice

Apple
Aloe Juice

Apple Juice Combinations

★ ✷ ✷

An apple a day keeps the doctor away!

Ingredients: Makes 2 Servings
(Agave syrup is optional.)

<Apple Kiwi Juice>

1 apple
1 kiwi
1½ tbsp. agave syrup

<Apple Grapefruit Juice>

1 apple
1 grapefruit
1½ tbsp. agave syrup

<Apple Pear Juice>

1 apple
1 pear
1½ tbsp. agave syrup

<Apple Aloe Juice>

½ cup aloe
1 apple
1 pear
1½ tbsp. agave syrup

Directions

<Apple Kiwi Juice>

1. Wash and cut apple into pieces.
2. Wash and peel kiwi and cut into pieces.
3. Press in this order—apple, kiwi, kale, celery.
4. Stir agave into finished juice.

<Apple Grapefruit Juice>

1. Wash and cut apple into pieces.
2. Peel grapefruit and cut into pieces.
3. Press in this order − apple, grapefruit.
4. Stir agave into finished juice.

<Apple Pear Juice>

1. Wash and cut apple and pear into pieces.
2. Press in this order—apple, pear.
3. Stir agave into finished juice.

<Apple Aloe Juice>

1. Wash aloe, apple and pear. Peel aloe and cut all into pieces.
2. Insert aloe into shoot along with apple and pear so mucilage can be easily extracted.
3. Stir agave into finished juice.

Carrot Mango Juice

★ ✬ ✬

Rich in vitamins, A, K and beta carotene this juice is a winner in nutrition and taste.

Ingredients:
Makes 2 servings

2 mangos
1 carrot
1½ tbsp. agave syrup
(If you prefer a sweeter juice.)

Directions

1. Wash and chop carrot into suitable pieces. Peel mango, remove seed and chop into pieces.

2. Press in this order—mango, carrot.

3. Stir agave into finished juice.

4. Serve.

Carrot Broccoli Juice

✦ ✧ ✧

So good, you'll forget it's good for you!

Ingredients:
Makes 2 servings

½ cup broccoli
pinch of salt (to blanch broccoli)
½ carrot
1 tomato
½ apple
1 banana
¾ cup milk
1½ tbsp. agave syrup

Directions

1. Wash and cut broccoli into pieces.
2. Fill a pot ⅔ full with water and pinch of salt and bring to a boil.
3. Add broccoli and blanch for approx. 3 minutes.
4. Set aside until cool.
5. Wash and chop carrot, apple and tomato into pieces.
6. Peel and slice banana.
7. Press in this order—broccoli, carrot, apple, tomato and banana.
8. Stir agave into finished juice.

Kiwi Cabbage Juice

★ ✷ ✷

Low in calories and sugar. This is what a diet drink should taste like.

Ingredients: Makes 2 servings

½ cup cabbage
6 kiwis
½ cup milk or soymilk
1½ tbsp. agave syrup

Directions

1. Wash and cut cabbage into pieces.

2. Fill a pot ⅔ full with water and pinch of salt and bring to a boil.

3. Add cabbage and blanch for approx. 2½ minutes.

4. Set aside and let cool.

5. Peel kiwi and cut into pieces.

6. Press in this order: kiwi, cabbage.

7. Stir milk and agave into finished juice.

Bell Pepper
Papaya Juice

Bell Pepper
Strawberry Juice

Bell Pepper & Strawberry Juice ★ ✭ ✭

Full of fiber and packed with vitamin C.
A unique alternative to O.J.

Bell Pepper Papaya Juice ★ ✭ ✭

An exotic way to spice up your day!

Ingredients: Makes 2 servings

½ bell pepper
30 strawberries
1½ tbsp. agave syrup

1 yellow bell pepper
1 papaya
1½ tbsp. agave syrup

Directions

1. Wash bell pepper, cut and remove stem and seeds. Chop into pieces.

2. Wash and hull strawberries.

3. Press in this order—Strawberries, bell pepper.

4. Stir agave into finished juice.

1. Wash bell pepper, cut and remove stem and seeds. Chop into pieces.

2. Peel papaya, remove seeds and cut lengthwise.

3. Press in this order—bell pepper, papaya.

4. Stir agave into finished juice.

Blueberry　　　　　　　　Basil

Cream Cheeses ✶ ✶ ✶

With **juice**presso, you can easily create endless fresh and nutritious flavor combinations. Your bagel never had it so good.

Ingredients: Makes 1 serving

Pick your flavor!
<Blueberry Cream Cheese>
10 blueberries → 1 tbsp. blueberry pulp

<Basil Cream Cheese>
¼ cup fresh basil → 1 tbsp. basil pulp

<Orange Almond Cream Cheese>
½ large. orange → 1 tbsp. orange pulp
1 tbsp. crushed almonds

<Strawberry Cream Cheese>
5 strawberries → 1 tbsp. strawberry pulp

<Basic>
3 tbsp. plain cream cheese

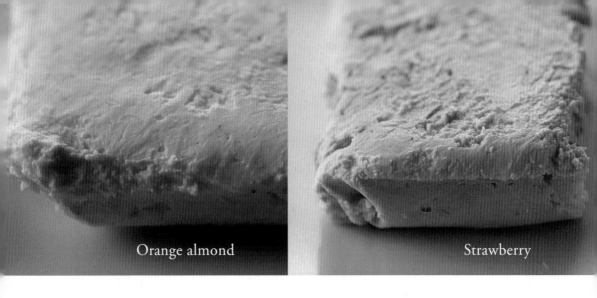

Orange almond   Strawberry

Directions

1. Remove cream from refrig–
   erator and allow to warm to
   room temperature.

2. Choose which cream cheese
   flavor you'd like, press the
   ingredients and gather the
   pulp.

3. Whip cream cheese until it
   becomes soft and pliable.
   Stir in pulp and any addi–
   tional ingredients.

4. Serve chilled.

Tip

Juice the basil with a bit of water to make clean up easier.

Tomato
Omelet

Quiche

Frittata

Tomato & Spinach Omelet

★ ★ ☆

A nutritionally complete breakfast that's completely delicious!

Ingredients: Makes 1 serving

2 large eggs
1 tomato → 3¼ tbsp. tomato pulp
¼ cup spinach → 2 tsp. spinach pulp
pinch of salt & pepper
1 tbsp. of olive oil

Directions

1. Wash, chop and press tomato and spinach. Put juice in an airtight container and store in the refrigerator for use in a juice recipe. Gather pulp.

2. Beat eggs in a small bowl.

3. Add oil to a skillet and heat on high.

4. Add eggs then add tomato and spinach pulp to one side of the egg.

5. Season with salt and pepper.

6. When approximately 80% cooked, fold over the empty side of the eggs to cover spinach and tomato.

7. Remove from heat when fully cooked and serve.

Frittatas

✳ ✳ ✳

You can give this Italian dish your own healthy, gourmet touch with **juice**presso.

Ingredients: Makes 3 servings

¼ cup mixed vegetable pulp
½ tomato → 2 tsp. tomato pulp
½ carrot → 2 tsp. carrot pulp
¼ cup spinach → 2 tsp. spinach pulp
1/8 cup celery → 2 tsp. celery pulp
½ cucumber → 2 tsp. cucumber pulp

\<Basic Frittata\>

5 eggs
½ cup milk
¼ cup cooked bacon pieces
¼ cup chopped mushrooms
1 tbsp. onion
1 tsp. chopped garlic
1 tbsp. olive oil
pinch of salt & pepper
3 tbsp. parmesan cheese
2 tsp. basil flakes

Directions

1. Press tomato, carrot, spinach, celery and cucumber. Store juice in an airtight container in the refrigerator. Gather the pulp.
2. In a bowl, whisk eggs, milk, salt, and pepper until salt dissolves.
3. Chop bacon and mushrooms into cubes and mince onions.
4. Add oil to pan and heat to high.
5. Add bacon, onions and mushroom to the pan and cook until the bacon is almost browned. Add pulp and garlic. Cook until pulp is softened and bacon and garlic are brown.
6. Remove from heat. Add the bacon, onions, mushrooms and garlic to the egg mixture. Stir gently.
7. Clean pan and add 1 tbsp. olive oil to the pan and heat to medium.
8. Add egg mixture to pan, reduce heat to low. Cook approximately 5 minutes or until eggs are firm.
9. Add cheese and remove from heat once cheese melts.
10. Garnish with basil flakes. Serve and enjoy!

Quiche

★ ★ ★

Served hot or cold any time of day, this French dish is as versatile as the combinations you can create with your **juíce**presso.

Ingredients: Makes 1 serving

¼ cup mixed vegetable pulp
½ cup onion → 1½ tbsp. onion pulp
2 tbsp. carrot → 2 tsp. carrot pulp
2 tbsp. potato → 2 tsp. potato pulp ½ apple → 2 tsp. apple pulp

<The Fillings>
2 eggs
½ cup fresh cream
1½ tbsp. plain yogurt
½ cup milk
pinch of salt & pepper
1 Store bought piecrust

Directions

1. Wash, chop and press the vegetables. Store the juice in an airtight container and refrigerate. Gather pulp.

2. Add oil to a skillet and heat to high.

3. Add pulp and cook until tender. Remove from heat.

4. Whisk all fillings together in a bowl.

5. Stir in pulp.

6. Bake the pie crust for 5 minutes at 350 degrees.

7. Remove from the oven add all ingredients and return to the oven.

8. Bake for approximately 20 minutes or until eggs spring back.

Potato Apple Soup

The hearty and filling soup is simple and quick. It makes eating healthy, easy.

Ingredients: Makes 1 serving

3 potatoes
1 onion
1 apple
1 ½ cups milk
2 tbsp. whipped cream
1 cup chicken stock
3 tsp. butter
pinch of salt & pepper
1 tbsp. flour (Add according to consistency preference.)

Directions

1. Wash and potato and apple. Peel potato and onion. Chop all into large cubes. Press. Add liquid to a large pot. Put pulp in an airtight container and store in the refrigerator for use at a later time.

2. Add milk, whipped cream, chicken stock and flour. Continuously stir while adding to smooth lumps. On low heat, bring mixture to a boil.

3. Strain mixture through a sieve to remove any solids. Add liquid back into the pot. Bring to a boil again over medium heat. Add butter and season with salt and pepper.

4. Remove from heat, pour into serving bowl, garnish with sliced apples and serve.

Autumn Squash Cream Soup ★ ✫ ✫

A warm and savory fall soup that's delightful year round.

Ingredients: Makes 1 serving

2¼ cups autumn squash
2¼ cups onion
¾ cup milk
¼ cup fresh cream or whipping cream
½ tbsp. olive oil
pinch of salt and pepper

Directions

1. Peel squash and cut into pieces. Peel and chop onion to equal size. Press.

2. Heat juice, pulp and milk on medium heat. Slowly add cream till desired concentration is reached. (Add additional cream for a creamier texture) Heat until mixture simmers.

3. Strain mixture. Add liquid back to pot, add olive oil and heat again until it becomes thick. Season with salt and pepper.

4. Whisk in remaining cream until foamy.

5. Remove from heat, pour into a bowl, garnish with salt and pepper.

Blueberry Pancakes

★ ★ ☆

A breakfast classic made deliciously healthy with **juice**presso.

Ingredients: Makes 2 servings

¾ cup blueberries
3¼ tbsp. sugar
2 eggs
½ cup milk
¾ cup pancake mix
1 tsp. butter

Directions

1. Press blueberries. Add juice and sugar to saucepan and cook over high heat, stirring constantly, until thick. Remove from heat and set aside.

2. Prepare pancake mix as directed on box. Stir in blueberry pulp.

3. Oil or butter skillet heat over medium. Pour mix in 4in diameter circles.

4. Wait for bubbles to form and pop then flip. Repeat until pancake batter is gone.

5. Top with the homemade blueberry sauce and serve.

Spinach Bread

★ ★ ☆

Using this bread to build your sandwich is a fresh way to add fiber and vitamin C to your meal.

Ingredients: Makes 4 servings

2 cups spinach → ½ cup spinach pulp
½ cup milk
1¼ cups strong flour or bread making flour
½ tbsp. dry yeast
½ tbsp. salt
1 tbsp. sugar
¾ tbsp. butter

Directions

1. Preheat oven to 325 degrees. Press spinach and add juice and milk together.

2. Add yeast, salt, sugar and flour to a bowl. Stir in juice and milk mixture till absorbed. Knead the dough until it become pliable then add butter. Knead again.

(Approximately 20 minutes by hand 6 minutes with mixer and dough hook on medium speed.)

3. Cover the dough with plastic wrap or wet cotton cloth and wait for it to rise. This is done at room temperature. Do not refrigerate. Takes approxi-

mately 1½ hours or until it is 3 times it's original size. Place it on a plate or pan and let it rest (approximately 30 minutes). It will rise and swell again.

4. Bake for 20 minutes in a bread loaf pan.

Lemon Custard

Pineapple-Rhubarb Jam

Lemon Custard ★ ✰ ✰

A tart treat on it's own or add it to recipes for a creamy zing.

Pineapple-Rhubarb Jam ★ ★ ✰

Wake up your toast with this unexpected jam packed with antioxidants and fiber.

Ingredients: Makes 4 servings

6 lemons
4 eggs
4 egg yolks
½ cup sugar
¼ cup butter

½ cup rhubarb stalks (frozen or fresh)
½ cup pineapple
1 cup sugar
¼ cup white wine
½ tbsp. lemon

Directions

1. Peel lemon and slice into 4 segments. Press.

2. Combine sugar, egg and egg yolk and whip. Add lemon juice to mixture and pour into a saucepan. Heat on medium−low until mixture thickens.

3. Melt butter then add to mixture in the saucepan. Stir until completely blended.

4. Remove from heat, transfer to a dish or airtight container. Seal and refrigerate until ready to serve.

1. Remove rhubarb leaves and clean and cut stalks.

2. Peal, core and slice pineapple.

3. Press rhubarb stalks and pineapple and place juice and pulp in airtight containers and store in the refrigerator overnight to age.

4. In a large pot bring juice and ½ of the pulp to a boil over medium−low heat. Stir constantly until thick and smooth.

   * NOTE : Jam will become thicker as it cools so do not over cook.

5. Remove from heat and add remaining pulp to give the jam texture.

   * WARNING : Use only rhubarb stalks. Leaves are toxic and indigestible.

Tomato Basil Scone

★ ☆ ☆

A savory slant on a English breakfast standard.

Ingredients: Makes 4 servings

1 large tomato
6 leaves fresh basil
1 cup all purpose flour
¼ cup butter
¼ cup sugar
1¼ tsp. salt
1 tbsp. baking powder

Directions

1. Preheat oven to 350 degrees F.

2. Wash, chop and press tomato.

3. Finely chop the basil.

4. Combine flour, butter, sugar, salt and baking powder together in a large bowl. Make a course dough.

5. Add tomato juice, tomato pulp and basil to the dough and knead together.

6. Chill the dough in the refrigerator for 20 minutes to harden.

7. Remove from the refrigerator. Cut and shape dough into scones and arrange on a cookie sheet.

8. Bake for 20 minutes or until golden brown.

Tip

Knead dough only until powdered ingredients are absorbed. Over kneading will make the scones dry.

Kiwi Pineapple Juice

★ ✬ ✬

Try this sweet and delicious juice as a healthy alternative to conventional dessert choices.

Ingredients: Makes 2 servings

5 kiwis
¾ cup chopped pineapple
1½ tbsp. agave syrup (If you like a sweeter juice.)

Directions

1. Peel kiwi and cut into 4 pieces.

2. Peel and chop pineapple into chunks. (You may also use canned pineapple.)

3. Press fruit in this order: kiwi then pineapple.

4. Pour into a glass, garnish with a pineapple wedge.

5. Serve.

Tip

If using canned pineapple, use less sweetener.

Blueberry Banana Smoothie   ★ ★ ✫

Loaded with potassium and antioxidants, this high energy smoothie is the "go-to" choice for athletes.

Ingredients: Makes 2 servings

½ cup milk
¼ cup plain yogurt
1 banana
½ cup blueberries

Directions

1. Rinse blueberries and peel banana.

2. Combine milk, yogurt and banana together.

3. Scoop into **juíce**presso and juice.

4. Press blueberries.

5. Stir together, pour into a glass and serve.

Orange
Tomato Juice

Orange
Autumn Squash Juice

Orange
Melon Juice

Orange Juice Combinations

★ ★ ✮

Start your day with an eye–opening, immunity bolstering twist on O.J.

Ingredients: Makes 2 servings

<Autumn Squash Juice>

½ squash
1 orange
½ cup milk
½ tbsp. parmesan cheese

<Orange Tomato Juice>

3 tomatoes
2 oranges
¼ lemon

<Orange Melon Juice>

1 orange
½ melon

Directions

<Autumn Squash Juice>

1. Wash and cut squash in half and clean out interior.
2. Placed on a lightly greased cookie sheet and bake at 300 F open side down for 20 minutes. Remove from oven and allow to cool.
3. Peel orange and segment.
4. After squash is cool, juice along with milk.
5. Press orange.
6. Stir juices together, garnish with cheese, serve.

<Orange Tomato Juice>

1. Wash and peel tomato and cut into wedges.
2. Peel orange and segment.
3. Press orange, lemon and tomato.
4. Stir well, serve.

<Orange Melon Juice>

1. Peel orange and segment.
2. Peel and remove seed from melon. Cut into chunks.
3. Press orange then melon.
4. Stir well, serve.

Melon Banana Shake

★ ☆ ☆

This potassium filled juice is a perfect way to start your day.

Ingredients:
Makes 2 servings

½ melon
1 banana
½ cup milk
1 plain yogurt (6oz.)

Directions

1. Peel melon, remove seeds and cut into chunks.
2. Peel banana cut into chunks and mix with milk and yogurt.
3. Press melon then banana mixture.
4. Stir together and serve.

Pomegranate Black Cherry Juice ★ ✵ ✵

This uncommon juice is a tart and refreshing treat that will quickly become a family favorite.

Ingredients:
Makes 2 servings

1 pomegranate (Use seed only)
20 black cherries

Directions

1. Cut pomegranate in half remove seeds.

2. Wash cherries and remove stems.

3. Press pomegranate seeds then cherries.

4. Serve.

Tip

If you want a creamier texture add soy, almond or cows milk till desired consistency is reached.

Mango Fizz

Orange-berry
Wine Fizz

Lemon Fizz

Fresh Fruit Fizzes

★ ★ ☆

Cool, fruity, healthy and refreshing. Summer never tasted so delicious!

Ingredients: Makes 2 servings

<Mango Fizz>

5 mangos
½ cup tonic water
½ cup soda water
2 tbsp. agave syrup
½ cup ice

<Orange-berry Wine Fizz>

50 strawberries 1 orange
1½ tbsp. red wine
2 tbsp. agave syrup ½ cup tonic water
½ cup soda water
½ cup ice

<Lemon Fizz>

6 lemons
½ cup tonic water
½ cup soda water
2 tbsp. agave syrup
½ cup ice

Directions

<Mango Fizz>

1. Peel mango. Thinly slice 1/8 of the mango and set aside. Chop the rest into chunks and press.
2. Set aside ¼ cup of the mango juice. Place the remainder in the freezer.
3. Mix mango juice, tonic water, soda and agave. Pour over ice in a glass.
4. Spoon frozen mango into glass. Garnish with sliced mango and serve.

<Orange-berry Wine Fizz>

1. Wash and hull strawberries. Press. Set ¼ cup aside. Freeze the rest.
2. Peel and segment oranges. Press.
3. Mix orange juice, strawberry juice, red wine and agave syrup together. Add tonic water and soda water.
4. Pour mixture over glass with ice. Spoon frozen strawberry juice and serve.

<Lemon Fizz>

1. Half 1 lemon. Cut ½ into slices—leave rind on.
2. Peel and cut the remaining lemons. Press. Put ¼ cup aside and the rest into the freezer.
3. Mix lemon juice, agave syrup, tonic water and soda water. Pour over ice.
4. Spoon frozen lemons into mixture. Top with lemon slices and serve.

Tomato Lime Juice

The vegetable juice favorite, balanced with a touch of lime for a refreshing kick.

Ingredients: Makes 2 servings

4 tomatoes
1 lime
1½ tbsp. agave

Directions

1. Wash tomatoes and cut into pieces.

2. Peel lime and cut into 4 pieces.

3. Press tomato then lime.

4. Add agave to sweeten. Serve.

Grapefruit Pineapple Juice

★ ✧ ✧

The fresh bite of flavor in this glass of liquid energy, really gets you going.

Ingredients: Makes 2 Servings

2 grapefruits
½ pineapple

Directions

1. Peel grapefruit and cut into 8 pieces.
2. Peel and core pineapple and cut into chunks.
3. Press grapefruit then the pineapple.
4. Serve!

Tip

Add celery or parsley to add fiber and boost the nutrition content.

Creamy Carrot Soymilk Soup

★ ☆ ☆

This delectable soup is wholesome and perfect for those who are dairy free.

Ingredients: Makes 4 servings

¼ cup rice
½ cup tofu (hard)
2 carrots → ½ cup carrot pulp
1½ cup soymilk

Directions

1. Soak rice in water for 1 hour.
2. Crush tofu.

3. Press carrots. Gather pulp and seal juice in an airtight container and store in the refrigerator for use later.

4. In a saucepan on high heat, heat carrot pulp, rice, tofu and soymilk until grains are soft.
5. Remove from heat, transfer to bowl and serve.

Tip

This is a wonderful recipe for babies. Just completely soften the rice for easy digestion.

Broccoli Apple Soup

★ ☆ ☆

The enticing aroma of this soup is second only to its taste.

Ingredients: Makes 4 servings

½ cup rice
½ cup broccoli
1 apple
½ cup water
1 tsp. salt

Directions

1. Soak rice in the water for an hour. Blanch broccoli and cut apple into 4 pieces. Squeeze broccoli and apple together using **juice**presso.

2. Put juice, pulp, water and rice in a pot and boil it until the rice becomes soft.

Citrus Chicken

Lemon Chicken
Sandwich

Citrus Chicken ★ ★ ✿

The superb combination of sweet and sour make this recipe a stand out.

Ingredients: Makes 1 serving

2 mandarin oranges
3 boneless chicken breasts

<Chicken Seasoning>

2 tsp. salt
1 tsp. turmeric
1 ¼ tbsp. chili powder
1 tbsp. olive oil
1 tbsp. chopped shallot
1 tbsp. chopped ginger
¾ cup sugar
¾ cup rice wine
1 tsp. cilantro

Directions

1. Peel, cut in half and press mandarin oranges. Set juice and pulp aside.
2. On a plate, combine chili powder, turmeric and salt. Rinse and pat dry chicken. Lay chicken in seasonings to cover then turn over to cover the other side.
3. Heat oven to 375 F. Place chicken on a oiled pan and roast for 20 to 25 minutes.
4. In a skillet heat olive oil on med/high heat. Add shallots and ginger. Sauté until both are clear.
5. Add sugar, rice wine and mandarin juice. Cook down on medium heat then remove from heat. Add pulp.
6. Remove chicken from the oven and place on a serving platter. Pour ingredients from skillet over chicken, garnish with cilantro and serve.

Lemon Chicken Sandwich ★ ★ ✿

The days of hum−drum chicken sandwiches are over. Juicy and flavorful, this might be your new favorite lunch.

1 lemon
½ cup mayonnaise
3 pieces of bacon
½ tomato 2 pieces of multi grain bread
2 leaves of romaine lettuce
1 boneless chicken breast

<Chicken Marinade>

1tsp. chopped garlic
1/8 tsp. thyme
1 tsp. olive oil

<Sauce>

1 tbsp. mayonnaise
1 tsp. chopped chives
1 tsp. parmesan cheese
1 lemon
pinch of salt and pepper

1. Peel and cut lemon into 4 wedges. Press.
2. In a bowl mix juice and pulp with mayonnaise. Set aside.
3. Fry bacon in skillet until desired crispness.
4. Preheat oven to 325 F. On a plate combine garlic, thyme and olive oil. Rinse and pat dry chicken breast. Lay chicken on the plate of spices and coat. Flip chicken to coat other side.
5. Place chicken on an oiled pan and cooked for 15 to 20 minutes. (Until cooked through.)
6. Add Parmesan cheese, chives and salt and pepper to mayonnaise and juice mixture. Mix together.
7. Remove chicken from the oven and cool. Once cool, tear or chop into bite size pieces. Add chicken to mayo mixture.
8. Spoon chicken mixture onto one side of your bead. Place romaine, tomato and bacon on the other. Join the sides, cut diagonally and serve.

Grilled Vegetable Salad
with Black Soybean Dressing

✶ ✹ ✹

A unique salad that's fantastic served hot or cold.

Ingredients: Makes 1 serving

¼ cup romaine
1 tomato (in wedges)

<Vegetables for grill>

½ cup eggplant
½ cup pumpkin
½ bell pepper
pinch of salt and pepper

<Black soybean dressing>

¼ cup boiled black soybeans
2½ tbsp. milk
½ cup mayonnaise
½ tsp. sesame oil
½ tsp. apple cider vinegar
1 tsp. mustard
pinch of salt and pepper
2 tbsp. honey

Directions

1. Boil black soybeans on high heat until softened. Remove from heat and cool.

2. Press soybeans and milk. In a bowl mix juice, pulp and other dressing ingredients. Set aside.

3. Thinly slice eggplant and pumpkin. (A peeler will work well). Chop bell pepper into lengthwise pieces. Add all to a skillet with a bit of olive oil. And salt and pepper. Stir fry until softened.

4. Rinse romaine and cut into "salad sized" pieces arrange in a salad bowl.

5. Top with stir-fried vegetables and drizzle with dressing. Garnish with tomato wedges and serve.

Tip

When juicing the soybeans and milk, add ingredients incrementally to avoid any blockages.

Hamburgers

✦ ✦ ✧

An American standard gets a serious, healthy upgrade courtesy of **juíce**presso.

Ingredients: Makes 1 serving

1 large carrot → 1¼ tbsp. carrot pulp

2 celery stalks → 2 tsp. celery pulp

¼ cup spinach → 2 tsp. spinach pulp

2 eggs

pinch of salt and pepper

¾ cup ground beef

¾ cup ground pork

2 tbsp. chopped onion

3¼ tbsp. breadcrumbs

Directions

1. Press carrots, celery and spinach. Put juice in an airtight container and store in the refrigerator for use at a later time. Gather pulp.
2. In a mixing bowl, whisk the eggs; add vegetable pulp, beef, pork and onions. Knead together. Add breadcrumbs bit by bit till you reach desired texture.
3. Shape approximately 3 tbsp. of the mixture into a patty.
4. Add oil to a skillet and heat to medium high. Add the patties and cook until desired temperature is reached.
5. Serve on a bun, on a salad or alone with your favorite condiments.

Tip

Uncooked patties can be store in an airtight container in the freezer for use at a later time.

Meatballs

✷ ✷ ✷

As a stand alone entrée or added to your favorite Italian dish, this recipe is "delizioso".

Ingredients: Makes 1 serving

1 large carrot → 1½ tbsp. carrot pulp
2 celery stalks → 2 tsp. celery pulp
1 small onion → 1½ tbsp. onion pulp
3 leaves fresh basil
1 egg
¾ cup ground beef

2 tbsp. bread crumbs
2 tsp. crushed garlic
1tsp. worcestershire sauce
3 tsp. fresh parsley pinch of salt
and pepper

Directions

1. Wash and chop carrot and celery, peel and chop onion. Press. Store juice in an airtight container to use at a later date. Gather pulp.

2. Wash and thinly julienne basil. In a small bowl, beat the egg.

3. In a large mixing bowl combine ground beef, vegetable pulp, egg, garlic, parsley, salt and pepper. Stir together. Slowly add breadcrumbs in and knead together.

4. Preheat oven to 350F. Roll mixture into a balls using 1½ tbsp. Place on a greased baking sheet. Bake in the oven until thoroughly cooked. Do not overcook or burn.

5. Serve as an entrée or add to your favorite Italian dish.

Kale Pasta

Spinach
Ravioli

Vegetable
Lasagna

Vegetable Lasagna

This Northern Italian dish is a mouthwatering way to get more vegetables into your family's diet.

Ingredients: Makes 2 servings

2 carrots → 1½ tbsp. carrot pulp
3 celery stalks → 2 tsp. celery pulp
½ apple
½ cup spinach → 2 tbsp. spinach pulp
pinch of salt and pepper
5 lasagna noodles
¾ cup meat sauce
2 tbsp. béchamel sauce
½ cup mozzarella

Directions

1. Preheat oven to 350F.
2. Wash carrot, celery, apple and spinach. Press. Store juice in an airtight container and refrigerate for use at a later date. Gather pulp.
3. Heat 1 tbsp. oil in a skillet on medium high. Add pulp, season with salt and pepper and stir—fry until soft.
4. Boil water in a large pot. Cook lasagna noodles until noodles are al dente.
5. Arrange lasagna noodles on the bottom of a greased baking pan. Spread meat sauce, béchamel sauce and cheese over the top. Add another layer of noodles. Spoon vegetable mixture on top then another layer of noodles. Repeat. Approximately 5 layers. Top with mozzarella.
6. Bake in oven for 30 minutes.
7. Serve hot.

Tip

Other green vegetables may be used instead of spinach, kale, broccoli, etc. according to your taste preference.

Spinach Ravioli

★ ★ ⚝

An Italian delicacy! Hearty, fresh and flavorful just as it was meant to be with **juíce**presso.

Ingredients: Makes 1 serving

<Ravioli filling>

1 ¼ tbsp. ricotta cheese
½ cup spinach → 2 tbsp. spinach pulp
pinch of salt and pepper

<Basic Recipe>

¼ cup ravioli dough (Make your own or store bought.)
1 egg yolk
2 tbsp. garlic
½ tsp. chives
1 tbsp. olive oil
1 can manila clams → 6 oz.
1 tsp. white wine
½ cup tomato sauce

Directions

1. Press spinach. Store juice in an airtight container in the refrigerator for use at a later date. Gather pulp.
2. Mix ricotta cheese with pulp and season with salt and pepper.
3. Spread egg yolk on one side of ravioli dough. Spoon on filling, fold over and press with fork to shape.
4. Mince garlic and finely chop the chives.
5. Cook ravioli in boiling water for 3 minutes or until they float. Gently drain.
6. Heat olive oil in a skillet on medium high heat. Add garlic and cook until lightly browned. Add claims and stir−fry for 3 to 4 minutes. Pour in white wine, cover and cook for 5 minutes.
7. Uncover, add tomato sauce, ravioli then gently stir in chives as not to damage the ravioli. Once the sauce thickens, remove from heat and serve.

Kale Pasta
(Must have a pasta machine)

★ ★ ☆

Kale, the super food, makes this pasta dish stupendous.

Ingredients: Makes 1 serving

½ cup kale
1¼ cup hard flour (bread flour)
2 eggs
2 tbsp. olive oil
1½ tbsp. extra virgin olive oil
2 tbsp. chopped garlic
¼ cup chicken stock
2 tsp. grated parmesan
pinch of salt and pepper

Directions

1. Wash and cut kale into pieces (size that will easily fit into feeding shoot). Press.

2. In a mixing bowl combine hard flour, egg, kale juice and olive oil. Knead together.

3. Place in refrigerator for 30 minutes.

4. Put kale pasta dough into pasta machine to make fettuccini noodles.

5. Bring a pot of salted water to a boil, add noodles and cook for approximately 7 minutes.

6. Put olive oil into a skillet and heat to medium high. Add garlic and cook until golden brown. Pour in chicken stock and cook down.

7. Add noodles into skillet and coat with contents. Remove from heat, transfer to plate top with Parmesan and serve.

All the Berries Sherbet ✶ ✶ ✶

A cool treat that is low in fat and sugar while bursting with antioxidants and flavor.

Ingredients: Makes 4 servings

¼ cup blackberries
¾ cup raspberries
½ cup strawberries
¼ cup blueberries
1½ cup fresh cream
½ cup milk
¼ cup honey
½ cup condensed milk

Directions

1. Mix berries with fresh cream, milk, honey and condensed milk together.

2. Press.
3. Mix juice and pulp together and put into an airtight container and freeze.

4. Remove from freezer and allow to warm slightly for easier serving.

Tip

Frozen berries can be used instead of fresh with the same results. Just allow berries to thaw prior to juicing.

Blueberry Jam & Mousse

★ ★ ☆

A scrumptious way to capture the all flavor and benefits of antioxidant rich blueberries.

Ingredients: Makes 4 servings

<Blueberry Jam>

1¼ cup blueberries
¾ cup sugar
3 tbsp. water
1 Lemon → 2½ tsp. lemon juice

<Blueberry Mousse>

1½ tsp. gelatin
½ cup blueberry jam
1¼ tsp. milk
½ cup whipped cream
½ cup plain yogurt

Directions

<Blueberry Jam>

<Blueberry Mousse>

1. Wash and press blueberries
2. Put juice, pulp and sugar into a sauce pan on the stove and bring to a boil. Reduce to about 1/3 the amount. Add lemon juice and continue to boil down.

3. Spoon into a container and chill.

1. Soak gelatin in cold water. Warm the jam and milk in a double boiler to soften. Add gelatin and melt.
2. In a bowl whisk whipped cream add mixture from the stove and mix. Spoon into preferable mold (mousse cups) refrigerate to harden then serve.

Tip

The jam is ready when amount reduces by half. Although it may look thin, it will thicken as it cools. Do not overcook.

Pear Pudding

✦ ✦ ✧

A simple yet elegant recipe that looks and tastes like you spent hours preparing it.

Ingredients: Makes 4 servings

1 pear
¼ cup milk
2 eggs
1 egg yolk
¾ cup sugar
3 tbsp. cornstarch
2 tsp. all purpose flour

Directions

1. Preheat oven to 300F.

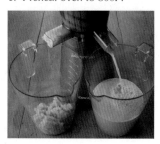

2. Wash and chop pear. Press with milk.

3. In a bowl, combine egg, egg yolk, sugar, pear juice/milk mixture and pear pulp. Add starch and flour, mix.

4. Fill ramekins ¾ full and bake in the oven for 30 minutes.

5. Remove from the oven. Allow to cool, transfer to the refrigerator to chill. Garnish with sliced pear and serve.

Banana Pound Cake

★ ✷ ✷

The aroma of this cake baking is heavenly. Homemade, made easy with **juíce**presso.

Ingredients: Makes 4 servings

1 tsp. baking soda
1 ½ tsp. baking powder
1 cup all purpose flour
4 bananas ¼ cup milk
½ cup softened butter
½ cup sugar
2 eggs
1 tsp. vanilla extract
½ tsp. cinnamon
½ tsp. salt

Directions

1. Preheat oven to 350F.

2. Grease bread loaf pan.

3. In a mixing bowl combine flour, baking soda, and salt.

4. Peel and cut the banana into chunks, mix with milk and press.

5. In a separate bowl, combine milk and banana juice with butter, sugar, vanilla extract and pulp. Stir well. Slowly add in eggs one at a time. Once thoroughly mixed, add in flour, baking soda and salt mixture. Mix the dough gently add in cinnamon.

6. Put into oven in the greased pan and bake for 30 minutes.

Tip

Bananas do not juice well alone. Press them with milk to prevent blockages.

Honey Beet Muffins

★ ✩ ✩

Subtle flavor and texture that's incomparably delicious.

Ingredients: Makes 4 servings

½ cup all purpose flour
1 tbsp. coco powder
¼ cup ground almonds
½ cup butter
2 eggs
½ cup sugar
2 tbsp. honey
1 tsp. vanilla extract
2 beets → ½ cup beet pulp

Directions

1. Press beets. Store juice in an airtight container and refrigerate for use at a later time. Gather pulp.

2. Preheat oven to 350F.

3. In a small bowl mix flour, coco powder, and the ground almonds together.

4. In a saucepan, melt and lightly brown butter,

5. In a large bowl add sugar honey, vanilla extract and stir together. Slowly mix in the egg. Once evenly distributed, add in the flour mixture and butter.

6. Lastly, add in beet pulp and knead together.

7. Fill greased muffin tins ¾ full and bake for 15 minutes or until muffin spring back when touched.

DINNER PARTY MENU
juicepresso

With **juice**presso, preparing a creatively unique, delectable and nutritious affair is a piece of cake!

Drink

Bell Pepper Strawberry Juice – Page 32
A sweet & tart, non-alcoholic people pleaser.

Lime Mojito – Page 94
Cool and refreshing, this drink is a party staple.

Appetizer

Lemon Ginger Salad Dressing – Page 146
An easy, tasty dressing. Ideal for almost any salad.

Potato Apple Soup – Page 40

Hearty, delicious and nutritious.

Main Course

Beef Fillet with Pomegranate Sauce – Page 108

The exotic flavor makes this dish distinctive and your party memorable.

Dessert

Pomegranate Coconut Jello – Page 122

Light and sweet. A perfect palate cleanser.

Coconut Cake – Page 158

A scrumptious finish to the perfect meal.

Pomegranate Martini - cocktail ✱ ✱ ✱

Restorative pomegranate gives the classic martini a chic and beneficial update.

Ingredients: Makes 3-4 servings

1 pomegranate
½ cup raspberries → ¼ cup raspberry juice
3 tbsp. water
1 orange → ¼ cup orange juice
2 oz. raspberry vodka
1 oz. grenadine
½ cup ice

Directions

1. Cup pomegranate in half and remove the seeds and press.

2. Wash raspberries and press raspberries and water to-gether to avoid blockages. Peel orange, segment and press.

3. Seal pulp in an airtight container and store in the refrigerator for use at a later time.

4. Add juice to a shaker of ice along with vodka and grenadine. Shake, strain into a martini glass, garnish with a few grenadine seeds and serve.

Lime Mojito - cocktail

✷ ✷ ✷

Ernest Hemingway's favorite libation done the **juice**presso way.

Ingredients: Makes 2 servings

4 mint leaves
½ lemon
2 limes
1½ tbsp. agave syrup
1½ oz. gold rum
5 oz. tonic Water
1/2 cup of ice

Directions

1. Wash and pat mint leaves dry. Tear leaves into small pieces. Peel lemon cut into quarters. Peel 1 lime and cut into quarters. Cut the other lime in half – width wise and slice into flat rings (for garnish). Peel the other half and cut to fit into feeding shoot. Press peeled lemon and limes.

2. Put pressed lemon and lime juice into a glass, add mint leaves and agave syrup, stir well. Pour in rum, ice and tonic water. Garnish with sliced limes and serve.

Berry Berry ✦ ✦ ✧
Margarita - cocktail

A berry fresh turn on a Mexican classic.

Ingredients:
Makes 2 servings

30 strawberries
½ cup blueberries
1 orange
½ oz. tequila
½ oz. triple sec.
¾ oz. agave syrup

Directions

1. Wash strawberries, remove stalks and cut in half. Peel oranges, Wash blueberries and raspberries. Press all, beginning with the strawberries.

2. Add tequila, triple sec and agave syrup. Stir together. Pour over a glass of crushed ice and serve.

Drinkable
Apple Pie - cocktail

★ ★ ⚝

Perfect on hot summer's day or a cold winter's night.

Ingredients:
Makes 2 servings

1 apple
½ oz. agave syrup
3 oz. apple cider
¾ oz. whiskey
1 cinnamon stick

Directions

1. Wash apple cut into 6 pieces. (Remove seeds.) Press.
2. Put apple juice into a glass or mug stir in whiskey, agave, and apple cider. (If you'd like to serve it hot, heat apple cider before adding.)
3. Garnish with a cinnamon stick and serve.

Strawberry Daiquiri - cocktail

★ ✦ ✦

Cool and refreshing, the daiquiri is always a crowd−pleaser.

Ingredients: Makes 2-3 servings

30 strawberries
½ lime
½ lemon
1½ tbsp. agave syrup
½ oz. rum
1½ lemon flavored carbonated water

Directions

1. Wash strawberries and remove stalk. Press.

2. Peel and press lemon and lime.

3. Stir in agave syrup, carbonated water and rum.

4. Pour over a glass of crushed ice and serve.

Green Grape - ade

★ ✭ ✭

A cool and bubbly thirst quencher.

Ingredients: Makes 2 servings

50 green seedless grapes
½ oz. agave syrup
5 oz. carbonated water
1 cup finely crushed ice

Directions

1. Wash grapes and remove stems. Press.

2. Stir in agave syrup and carbonated water.

3. Serve over a glass of finely crushed ice.

Mango-rita - cocktail

A party staple in an unexpected flavor. The Mango–rita is destined to be the new "it" drink!

Ingredients: Makes 2 servings

4 mangos
1 lime
1 cup finely crushed ice
½ oz. tequila
½ oz. triple sec

Directions

1. Peel mango, cut in half lengthwise and remove seeds. Press. (Set aside a few slices for garnish.)

2. Peel and cut lime into 4 pieces. Press.

3. Stir agave, tequila, lime and triple sec into juice.

4. Pour into glass over crushed ice. Garnish with sliced mango and serve.

Cherry Lemon Cooler

★ ✬ ✬

Tangy—tart cherries contain melatonin so this drink refreshes and relaxes.

Ingredients: Makes 2 servings

12 cherries
½ lemon
1 cup ice
5 oz. soda
½ oz. agave syrup

Directions

1. Wash and remove seeds and stems from cherries. Press.

2. Peel lemon, press.

3. Stir agave into the juices.

4. Pour juices over ice, top with soda, serve.

Tip

Add vodka to make it a cherry martini.

Cranberry
Sauce

Pomegranate
Sauce

Citrus
Dressing

Fresh Sauces

★ ★ ☆

Your creative dish possibilities are endless with these inspired sauces.

Ingredients:
Makes 2 servings

<Cranberry Sauce>
3½ oz. cherries
3½ tbsp. sugar
1½ oz. water
pinch of salt

<Pomegranate Sauce>
2 pomegranates
3 tbsp. balsamic vinegar
2 tbsp. butter

<Citrus Dressing>
1 lemon
1 lime
1 tbsp. olive oil
1 tbsp. honey
pinch of salt and pepper

Directions

<Cranberry Sauce>
1. Wash cranberries, remove stems and pits and press.
2. In a saucepan, heat the juice. Add sugar, water and salt and bring to a boil. Reduce heat, continue stirring until mixture thickens and reduces by half.
3. Remove from heat, chill and serve.

<Pomegranate Sauce>
1. Cut pomegranate into 4 pieces. Separate seeds and press.
2. Add juice to saucepan with balsamic vinegar and bring to a boil. Reduce heat and continue to stir until mixture thickens and is reduced by half.
3. Add butter and mix well. Serve warm or chilled.

<Citrus Dressing>
1. Peel lemon and lime cut into 4 pieces and press.
2. In a bowl combine juice, olive oil, honey and salt and pepper. Stir well before topping your favorite dish.

Beef Fillet with Pomegranate Sauce and Potatoes

✳ ✳ ✳

An exotic twist on an American standard.

Ingredients: Makes 1 serving

<Pomegranate Sauce>
Recipe on Page 110

<Tenderloin Marinade>
1 tbsp. chopped fresh rosemary
pinch of salt and pepper
5 tbsp. olive oil
7 oz. beef tenderloina
pinch of salt and pepper

<Potatoes>
10 oz. potatoes
2 tbsp. olive oil
pinch of salt and pepper

Directions

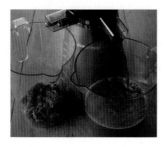

1. Make pomegranate sauce from page 107 and set aside.
2. Combine marinade ingredients in a sturdy 1-gallon, resealable plastic bag, add tenderloin and refrigerate. Allow to marinate for a minimum of 3 hours.

3. Pre-heat oven to 325F. Peel and chop potatoes, put in a bowl with olive oil and salt and pepper to coat. Transfer to cookie sheet bake for 20 to 25 minutes (until potatoes are soft).

4. In an oiled skillet, cook tenderloin on high heat until both sides are browned. Lower heat and cook until desired pinkness is reached.
5. Serve tenderloin topped with pomegranate sauce and the roasted potatoes.

King Prawns with Melons and Citrus Dressing

*juice*presso's cool and inventive spin on the shrimp cocktail.

Ingredients: Makes 1 serving

<Citrus Dressing>
Recipe on Page 107

<Basic>
10 oz. shrimp (Peeled and deveined.)
1 bay leaf
¼ cup sliced onions
3 peppercorns
¼ cup melon (honeydew or cantaloupe)
¼ cup watermelon

Directions

1. Prepare citrus dressing and set aside.
2. In a pot, boil water with peppercorns, bay leaf and onion. Add shrimp and cook until pink. Remove from water and chill.
3. Make ¼ cup of cantaloupe/honey dew balls and ¼ cups watermelon balls. Place in a serving dish, add chilled shrimp top with citrus dressing and serve chilled.

Tip

Do not top with dressing until you are ready to serve.

Avocado & Spinach Soup with Chili Shrimp

★ ★ ✯

Creamy and cool with a dash of spice, this soup hits all the right notes.

Ingredients: Makes 1 serving

2 avocados
3 oz. spinach
1½ cups chicken stock
1½ tsp. shallots
1tsp. olive oil
¾ cup whipping cream
pinch of salt and pepper

<Shrimp Marinade>
6 shrimp (Peeled and deveined.)
2 tsp. garlic
2 tsp. chili powder
¼ tsp. nutmeg

Directions

1. Peel Avocado, cut in half, remove seed and chop into cubes. Wash spinach, cut into "easy to feed" lengths. Press both with chicken stock.

2. In a skillet stir−fry shallots in oil until clear. Reduce to me−dium heat, add juiced mixture and whipping cream and cook for 10 minutes. Season with salt and pepper, remove from heat and allow to cool.

3. Wash and peel shrimp. In a resealable plastic bag, mari−nade shrimp with garlic and chili powder for 30 minutes.

Heat a skillet with a bit of oil, and add shrimp. Stir−fry on high until shrimp are pink (completely cooked). Remove from heat and allow to cool.

4. Pour avocado mixture into a bowl, top with shrimp, sprin−kle with nutmeg and serve.

Tip

This soup may be served hot or cold.

Grissini with Prosciutto & Fruit Dip ★ ✩ ✩

Give your finger food appetizers a dignified revamp with **juice**presso!

Ingredients: Makes 1 servings

\<Fruit Dip\>
1 orange
1 banana
6 oz. plain yogurt
1 tsp. honey
4-6 grissini (breadsticks)
4-6 thinly sliced prosciutto

Directions

1. Peel orange and segment. Peel banana and chop into chunks. Press banana then orange.

2. Mix juice and pulp together, stir in yogurt and honey. Chill.

3. Wrap prosciutto around grissini and place on serving dish. Put dipping sauce into a small bowl and serve.

Red Melon Gazpacho

Too hot to cook? This summer soup is simple, delish and ready in a flash.

Ingredients: Makes 1 serving

1½ cups seedless watermelon
½ cups cantaloupe
1 lime
1 red bell pepper
3 tsp. crushed garlic
1 oz. water
½ tbsp. olive oil
pinch of salt and pepper
dash of dill

Directions

1. Peel melon and cut into chunks. Peel lime and cut into 4 pieces. Wash and chop bell pepper. Press all.

2. Peel and chop garlic. Add garlic into juice and mix thoroughly. Strain mixture into a bowl, add water and season with salt and pepper.

3. Chill soup in the refrigerator for 30 minutes, top with dill and serve.

Melon Soup with Prosciutto wrapped Grissini

★ ✦ ✦

Melons and mint are a divine combo in this decidedly summer soup.

Ingredients: Makes 1 serving

½ cup honeydew
2 tsp. apple mint
3 tsp. melon liquor
½ lime
2 tsp. sugar
1 oz. cantaloupe
I grissini (breadstick)
1 thinly sliced piece of prosciutto

Directions

1. Peel and remove seeds from honeydew. Chop into chunks. Peel lime and cut into 4 pieces. Wash and pat dry the honey mint. Press all together.

2. Add melon liquor and sugar into juice. Stir well until sugar dissolves. Chill.

3. Using a melon baller, create 5 or 6 balls from the cantaloupe. Coil prosciutto around grissini.

4. Pour chilled soup into a bowl, add cantaloupe balls, garnish with prosciutto grissini, and serve.

Green Grape Popsicle

A refreshing and unique adult treat that can be made for children by simply removing the alcohol.

Ingredients: Makes 4 servings

1¼ cup green seedless grapes
1 lemon
1 cup chardonnay wine
½ cup sweetener (agave, sugar, sugar substitute)

Directions

3. Add the whole grapes into mixture, pour into popsicle molds and freeze.
4. Serve once completely frozen.

1. Wash green grapes and remove stems. Peel and cut lemon into 4 segments. Press both. (Leave a few grapes whole to put into the bars.)

2. Stir in chardonnay and sugar into juice until sugar dissolves.

Pomegranate Coconut Jello

★ ★ ★

Fruity, nutty, creamy and yummy!

Ingredients: Makes 4 servings

<Coconut Jello>
½ tbsp. gelatin
½ cup coconut milk
2½ tbsp. sugar
½ cup plain yogurt

<Pomegranate Jello>
½ tbsp. gelatin
4 pomegranates → 9 oz pomegranate juice
1 lemon
2½ tbsp. sugar

Directions

1. Cut pomegranate in half and scoop out the seeds. Peel lemon and cut into 4 seg-ments. Press pomegranate seed and lemon.

2. Warm coconut milk in a saucepan over medium heat. Add in sugar and stir until dissolved.

3. Dissolve the gelatin for the coconut Jello ¼ cup cold water.

4. Stir in the gelatin into the coconut milk mixture in the saucepan until the gelatin melts.

5. Remove from heat and mix with the plain yogurt.

6. Pour into dessert glasses ⅓ full and refrigerate for 1 hour to set.

7. Heat pomegranate juice and lemon juice in a saucepan on medium high heat. Add in sugar and stir until dissolved.

8. Dissolve the gelatin for the coconut Jello ¼ cup cold water.

9. Stir in the gelatin into the pomegranate and lemon juice mixture in the saucepan until the gelatin melts.

10. Remove from heat and pour mixture on top of firmed coconut gelatin mixture to fill the dessert glasses.

11. Refrigerate for 2 hours.

12. Serve cold.

Tip

To make a two layer dessert, pour the pomegranate Jello on top of the coconut Jello only after the coconut Jello has chilled firm.

Orange Hazelnut Brownie Tart

★ ★ ★

This delightful combination bring out the best in both flavors.

Ingredients: Makes 4 servings

<Shortbread Pastry>

¾ cup all purpose flour
1½ tbsp. ground almonds
2½ tbsp. powdered sugar
½ cup butter
1 small egg

<Orange Brownie>

2 oranges
½ cup brown sugar
½ cup dark baking chocolate
2½ tbsp. butter
½ cup all purpose flour 1 tbsp. cocoa powder
1 tbsp. baking powder
3 eggs
¼ cup finely hopped hazelnuts

Directions

1. Mix flour, ground almonds and powdered sugar together. Add in cold butter and knead. Add in egg and continue to knead. Form into a ball and place in refrigerator 30 minutes to rise.

2. Remove pastry from refrigerator and break off sections and mold into the bottom of a muffin cups in a muffin pan. Refrigerate.

3. Preheat oven to 325F.

4. Peel and segment orange. Press.

5. Pour squeezed juice and pulp into a saucepan. Add brown sugar and heat on high until mixture thickens to a jam like consistency.

6. Melt chocolate and butter together in a double boiler.

7. In a bowl combine flour, cocoa powder and baking powder. Add eggs one at a time and stir. Slowly add boiled down orange mixture. Stir. Add in chocolate and butter mixture. Once all ingredients are combined, add in finely chopped hazelnuts and gently stir.

8. Pour into muffin cups on top of crust. Bake for 30 minutes or until muffins spring back when touched.

Citrus Jello

★ ★ ☆

The creative presentation and sweet and sour flavor makes this treat a winner with kids and adults alike.

Ingredients: Makes 4 servings

½ tbsp. gelatin
4 lemons
1 orange
½ cup sugar

Directions

1. Dissolve gelatin in ¼ cup cold water.

2. Cut lemons in half and scrape out. (Use peels as the dish). Press lemon scrapings.

3. Place juice into a saucepan and bring to a boil. Add in sugar and gelatin into saucepan and completely dissolve.

4. Place lemon peels on a plate. Remove juice mixture room heat and pour into lemon halves. Transfer to refrigerator to firm. Serve cold.

Part. 3
Diet & Beauty

Non-Fat Fruit Smoothie

★ ✧ ✧

Wholesome and brimming with flavor, you'll forget it's fat free.

Ingredients: Makes 2 servings

20 strawberries
½ pear
¾ cup non-fat milk
½ cup yogurt
½ banana

Directions

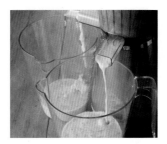

1. Wash strawberries and pear. Remove stalks and stem. Cut strawberries in half and cut pear into 8 pieces (remove seed).

2. Chop banana into chunks. Mix banana, milk and yogurt together. Press. Discard pulp.

3. Press strawberries. Combine strawberries and banana mixture together and serve.

Soymilk

★ ☆ ☆

Homemade soymilk tastes better, is better for you and is better on your budget than store bought.

Ingredients: Makes 4 servings

4¼ cups water
¾ cup soybeans

Directions

1. Rinse dry soybeans. Soak in water for at least 12 hours.

2. Boil soybeans in 4½ cups of water until softened. Remove from saucepan and refrigerate until cold.

3. Once soybeans are cold, press. You can sweetener to taste with honey, agave or maple syrup.

4. Serve cold.

Banana Pineapple
Soymilk Smoothie

Strawberry
Soymilk
Smoothie

Autumn Squash
Tofu Shake

Chocolaty Banana
Almond Soymilk Smoothie

Soymilk Shakes & Smoothies

★ ✬ ✬

The combinations and creations are as endless as your imagination.

Ingredients: Makes 2 servings

<Autumn Squash Tofu Shake>
½ autumn squash
¾ cup tofu
¾ cup soymilk (Recipe on page 133). ¼ cup yogurt
2 tbsp. sweetened condensed milk

<Chocolaty Banana Almond Soymilk Smoothie>
3 bananas
1½ cups soymilk (Recipe on page 133).
2 tsp. finely chopped raw almonds
1½ tbsp. chocolate syrup

<Strawberry Soymilk Smoothie>
30 strawberries
¼ cup raspberries
¾ cup soymilk (Recipe on page 133).

<Banana Pineapple Soymilk Smoothie>
1 banana
¾ cup soymilk (Recipe on page 133).
¾ cup chopped pineapple

Directions

<Autumn Squash Tofu Shake>
1. Preheat oven to 300F. Cut autumn squash in half. Place half on cookie sheet and bake for 20 minutes.
2. Allow to cool, scrape out the insides into a bowl. Add tofu, soymilk and yogurt and mix together. Press using your **juíce**presso.
3. Add condensed milk to pressed juice to sweeten and to reach desired consistency.
4. Serve cold.

<Chocolaty Banana Almond Soymilk Smoothie>
1. Peel and chop banana. Mix with ½ of the soymilk and press.
2. Mix the rest of the soymilk with your pressed mixture. Stir in almonds and chocolate syrup. Stir briskly.
3. Chill and serve cold.

<Strawberry Soymilk Smoothie>
1. Wash strawberries and raspberries. Remove stems from strawberries. Slice larger strawberries in half. Press strawberries.
2. Mix raspberries with milk. Press.
3. Add agave for added sweetness if needed.
4. Serve cold.

<Banana Pineapple Soymilk Smoothie>
1. Peel and chop banana. Mix with soymilk and press.
2. Press pineapple.
3. Mix and serve.

Tip

All may be served over or mixed with ice for added chill! You can also refrigerate your ingredients prior to pressing to produce cold shakes and smoothies without ice.

Kiwi Milk Shake

★ ☆ ☆

Filled with protein and vitamin C, this shake is as nutritious as it is delicious.

Ingredients: Makes 2 servings

5 kiwis
½ cup soymilk, almond milk or cows milk.
¼ cup yogurt
2 tbsp. sweetened condensed milk

Directions

1. Peel Kiwi and cut into 4 pieces.

2. Combine milk, condensed milk and yogurt. Stir in kiwi. Press.

3. Serve cold.

Banana
Cabbage
Soymilk

Banana Spinach
Soymilk

Banana Cabbage Soymilk ★ ✩ ✩

Low calorie and a low glycemic index make this an ideal diet drink.

Banana Spinach Soymilk ★ ★ ✩

An unequaled drink for skin and beauty maintenance.

Ingredients: Makes 2 servings

< Banana Cabbage Juice>
1 banana
½ cup chopped cabbage
1 kiwi
¾ cup soymilk
1½ tbsp. agave syrup

< Banana Spinach Soymilk>
1 banana
1 cup spinach
¾ cup soymilk
2 tsp. agave syrup

Directions

< Banana Cabbage Juice>

1. Peel and chop banana.

2. Wash, dry and chop cabbage.

3. Peel and slice kiwi into 4 pieces.

4. Press 1,2 and 3 in order along with equal amounts of soymilk.

5. Stir in agave syrup to taste and serve.

< Banana Spinach Soymilk>

1. Peel and chop banana. Mix with ½ the soymilk and press.

2. Wash and chop spinach. mix with other ½ of the soymilk and press.

3. Mix together, stir in agave syrup and serve.

Celery Gazpacho

Refreshingly cold on hot summer days, this adaptation of the classic Spanish cold tomato soup is exquisite.

Ingredients: Makes 1 serving

¼ cup chopped celery
1 apple
¼ cup chopped onion
¼ cup chopped spinach
pinch of salt and pepper
sprinkle of cinnamon

Directions

1. Wash celery, apple and spinach and chop into suit—able pieces.

2. Blanch spinach. In a pan of water for 3 minutes.

3. Press all. Collect juice and refrigerate.

4. When well chilled, trans—fer to bowl. Stir in salt and pepper to taste, top with cinnamon and serve.

Tip

If you prefer more texture in your soup, add in a bit of pulp. This will also enhance the nutrition content.

Cucumber Yogurt

★ ✩ ✩

Low sugar, high protein, a sublime way to start your day!

Ingredients: Makes 1 serving

½ large cucumber → 2 tsp. cucumber pulp
¼ cup plain yogurt
½ lemon

Directions

1. Peel and chop ½ cucumber. (Peel may be left on if you pre–fer). Press and gather pulp.

2. Chop lemon in half, peel and press. Gather juice.

3. Mix 2 tsp. cucumber pulp and lemon juice into yogurt.

4. Chill well and serve.

Tip

To make a great facial mask, substitute aloe for the lemon. It soothes and reduces redness and puffiness.

Layered Vegetable Terrine

✱ ✱ ✱

The artistry of the assemblage makes this dish as much a feast for the eyes as for the palate.

Ingredients: Makes 2 servings

8 large beet greens or Swiss chard
6 large tomatoes → 1 cup tomato pulp
4 carrots → ½ cup carrot pulp
2½ potatoes → ½ cup potato pulp
3 Red peppers → ½ cup red pepper pulp
I cup English peas (fresh or thawed frozen may be used)
5 small eggs
1½ tbsp. olive oil
2¼ cups heavy cream
⅓ cup parmesan cheese

Directions

1. Bring a large pot of water to the boil. Salt it and blanch the beet greens for 1 minute. Remove the leaves and immediately rinse under ice−cold water to set their color. Gently lay flat on tea towels, and pat dry with another tea towel. They should be completely dry.

2. Line a buttered terrine mold with a piece of parchment. Neatly lay in the beet leaves to cover the bottom and sides completely. They should dangle over the sides a bit so that they can be folded over the completed terrine later.

3. Wash and chop all produce. Press and gather pulp.

4. Heat small amount of olive oil in a skillet. Add in tomato pulp, cook until softened and season with salt and pepper. Remove from heat and set aside.

5. Repeat step 4 with each vegetable. Allow all to cool.

6. Preheat the oven to 350F.

7. Beginning with the carrot, mix pulp with heavy cream and egg. Whisk together thoroughly then spoon into terrine mold. Distribute evenly.

8. Repeat process with each vegetable except the red pepper.

9. Whisk egg with parmesan and spoon into the terrine mold. The top layer will be the red pepper, heavy cream and egg mixture.

10. Fold the overhanging beet leaves over the top and bake in a water bath for 1 hour.

11. Remove from oven and allow it to cool completely. If possible, refrigerate overnight so it sets well.

12. Serve cold or chilled.

Tip

Cook grape juice and gelatin in a double boiler. Once it thickens, spread it out on a cookie sheet, in a thin layer to firm. Once it is firm, garnish the top of your dish. It will enhance the look of your dish as well as the taste.

Lemon Ginger Salad Dressing

★ ✵ ✵

Tart, zesty and full of zing this dressing works great with most everything!

Ingredients: Makes 1 serving

1 lemon → 2 tbsp. lemon juice
1½ ginger root → 1½ tbsp. ginger juice
1 tbsp. olive oil
3 tbsp. walnut oil
½ tbsp. sesame oil
1 tsp. honey
½ tsp. chopped parsley
1 tsp. salt
pinch of pepper

Directions

1. Peel and chop lemon and ginger. Press and gather juice.

2. Combine all ingredients in a bowl and mix well.

3. Transfer to salad dressing service vessel and refrigerate.

4. Serve on you favorite salad or dish!

Tomato Salsa

Bruschetta

Bruschetta ★ ⊹ ⊹

An Italian favorite done the *juice*presso way.

Ingredients: Makes 1 serving

\<Bruschetta>

½ cucumber → 1¼ tbsp. cucumber pulp
1 large tomato → 3½ tbsp. tomato pulp
½ tbsp. olive oil
pinch of salt and pepper
4 slices mozzarella
2 leaves basil
4 slices baguette
½ tbsp. balsamic reduction

Directions

\<Bruschetta>

1. Peel cucumber and chop into chunks. Press. Gather requested amount of pulp.
2. Wash and chop tomato. Press. Gather requested amount of pulp.
3. Place pulp into a bowl; add olive oil and salt and pepper. Gently stir.
4. Toast slices of baguette until brown. Allow to cool.
5. Place mozzarella onto toasted baguette and top with pulp mixture.
6. Top with torn basil and balsamic reduction.
7. Serve.

Tomato Salsa ★ ⊹ ⊹

\<Tomato Salsa>

2 large tomatoes
½ lemon
¼ red bell pepper
¼ green bell pepper
½ onion
½ tbsp. garlic
½ tbsp. cilantro
pinch of salt and pepper

\<Tomato Salsa>

1. Wash and cut each tomato into 4 pieces. Press. Collect both juice and pulp.
2. Peel lemon cut into pieces. Press. Collect only juice.
3. Wash and chop bell peppers. Press. Collect only the pulp.
4. Chop garlic, onion and cilantro.
5. Combine tomato juice and pulp, lemon juice, bell pepper pulp, onions, garlic and cilantro. Mix well. Season with salt and pepper to taste.
6. Chill and serve.

Stuffed Bell Pepper

✶ ✶ ⚹

Colorful, flavorful and healthful! Splendid as a side dish but hearty enough for a main course.

Ingredients: Makes 1 serving

<For Stuffing>
½ cup chopped onion
2 tbsp. corn
¼ cup chopped broccoli → 1 tbsp. broccoli pulp
¼ cup chopped cauliflower → 1 tbsp. cauliflower pulp
¼ cup chopped potato → 1 tbsp. potato pulp
¼ apple → 1 tbsp. apple pulp
¼ cup spinach → 1 tbsp. spinach pulp
pinch of salt and pepper

<Bell Pepper>
1 bell pepper
2 tbsp. mozzarella
1½ tbsp. olive oil

Directions

1. Wash and cut bell pepper in half and set aside.

2. Preheat oven to 350F.

3. Press all vegetables expect the onion and corn. Gather pulp.

4. Heat olive oil in a skillet; add onion corn and vegetable pulp and stir−fry.

5. Place bell pepper on a cookie sheet and spoon in mixture from the skillet. Top with mozzarella and sprinkle with olive oil.

6. Bake for 10 minutes.

7. Serve hot.

Caprese Basil Pesto

★ ✹ ✹

As a dip or bread topper it's unrivaled but you can also use it on your pasta as a contemporary departure from tomato sauce.

Ingredients: Makes 1 serving

¾ cup basil → 2 tbsp. basil pulp
¼ cup pine nuts
½ tbsp. sesame seeds
½ cup olive oil
pinch of salt

Directions

1. Press the basil and gather the pulp.

2. In a mixing bowl, combine basil pulp and all other ingredients.

3. Serve with sliced baguette for delicious appetizer or over pasta for a healthy main course.

Soymilk Tiramisu

★ ★ ✧

One taste and you'll fall in love with this decadent Italian dessert.

Ingredients: Makes 4 servings

<Soymilk Tiramisu Cream>
1 tsp. gelatin
¾ cup Soybeans → ¼ cup soybean pulp
1¼ cup mascarpone cheese
¼ cup soymilk
¼ cup sugar
¾ cup fresh cream

<Espresso Ladyfingers>
12 ladyfingers
½ cup espresso
½ cup sugar syrup (half sugar, half water)
½ tsp. cocoa powder

Directions

1. Dissolve gelatin a ¼ cup cold water.

2. Press soybean and collect the pulp.

3. In a bowl, combine soybean pulp, mascarpone cheese, and soymilk. Mix well. Continue stirring and add sugar. One completely absorbed, add 3½ tbsp. fresh cream and gelatin.

4. In a separate bowl, whip the remainder of the fresh cream. Little by little, add in the mixture in step 3. Whip until it forms a soft cream.

5. In a bowl mix ½ cup sugar and ½ cup water (sugar syrup). Dissolve completely and add in espresso. Dip ladyfingers into mixture until they are saturated.

6. In a dessert ramekin, layer ladyfingers with tiramisu cream. (Number of layers depends on depth of ramekin).

7. Transfer to refrigerator and chill for at least 2 hours.

8. Sprinkle with cocoa powder and serve cold.

Soymilk Cinnamon
Panna Cotta

Soymilk Coffee
Crème Brulee

Soymilk Cinnamon Panna Cotta

★ ✢ ✢

This creamy, Italian dessert is a heavenly finish to any meal.

Ingredients: Makes 4 servings

<Soymilk Cinnamon Panna Cotta>

soymilk cinnamon panna cotta
¾ tbsp. gelatin
1½ cups soymilk
½ cup maple or agave syrup
½ tsp. cinnamon powder
pinch of nutmeg

Soymilk Coffee Crème Brulee

★ ✢ ✢

Creme Brulee's seductive secret lies is in the contrast between the brittle caramelized topping and the smooth, creamy custard.

<Soymilk Coffee Crème Brulee>

¼ cup maple or agave syrup 4 egg yolks
1½ cups of soymilk
¼ cup espresso
1 cup heavy cream
pinch of sugar

Directions

<Soymilk Cinnamon Panna Cotta>

1. Dissolve gelatin in ¾ cup of cold water.
2. Heat soymilk in a saucepan to 100F. Stir in gelatin.
3. Continue stirring and add maple syrup and nutmeg.
4. Pour into dessert ramekins and harden in the refrigerator for at least 2 hours.
5. Sprinkle with cinnamon powder and serve.

<Soymilk Coffee Crème Brulee>

1. Preheat oven to 300F.
2. In a saucepan, heat soymilk to 100F.
3. In a mixing bowl beat egg yolk and maple syrup add heavy cream in a little at a time.

4. Make espresso.
5. Stir soymilk and espresso into egg yolk, cream and syrup mixture. Stir gently to avoid making foam.
6. Spoon mixture into dessert ramekins and place in baking pan.
7. Pour water into bottom of baking pan until it comes half way up the sides of the ramekins.
8. Bake for approximately 40 minutes until the crème brulee is set but still trembles in the middle.
9. Refrigerate for at least 2 hours.
10. Remove from refrigerator sprinkle with sugar and torch.
11. Serve.

Carrot Cake

The most luscious cake recipe made easy and healthy using your *juice*presso.

Ingredients: Makes 4 servings

<For Cake>

3 large eggs
1 cup sugar
¼ tsp. salt
¼ cup oil
½ cup all purpose flour
¼ tsp. baking soda
pinch of baking powder
4 large Carrots → ¾ cup pulp
2½ tbsp. walnuts coarsely chopped

<For Frosting>

¼ cup plain yogurt
½ cup cream cheese
3½ tbsp. powdered sugar
¼ tsp. vanilla extract

Directions

1. Preheat oven to 350F.
2. Wash and chopped carrot. Press. Collect pulp.
3. In a mixing bowl combine sugar and salt. Slowly add in eggs 1 at a time then add in oil.
4. In another bowl, combine flour, cinnamon, baking powder and baking soda. Slowly add into mixing bowl with sugar mixture continue mixing until powder is absorbed.
5. Add in carrot pulp and walnuts. Stir gently together.
6. Fill a greased cake pan ¾ full. Bake for 25 minutes or until cake spring back.
7. Remove from oven and allow to cool.
8. Soften cream cheese to room temperature.
9. In a mixing bowl combine cream cheese, yogurt, powdered sugar and vanilla extract. Whip until fluffy.
10. Top cooled cake with frosting.
11. Serve.

Avocado Pudding

★ ★ ☆

Delicate, creamy and delectable, it only seems unconventional until you try it.

Ingredients: Makes 4 servings

½ tsp. gelatin
2 avocados
1½ cup milk
¼ cup sugar

Directions

1. Soak gelatin in ¼ cup of cold water.

2. Peel avocado and remove seeds. Chop into chunks and press with 1 cup of milk.

3. Cook the remaining ½ cup of milk in a double boiler. Add in sugar and gelatin and stir until completely dissolved.

4. Mix pressed juice into the double broiler. Stir well.

5. Remove from heat and transfer to pudding cups and place in the refrigerator to cool and firm.

6. Serve cold.

Index

Juice

Dish

Dessert

Quick & Healthy

Daily **juice**presso

Smart Extraction System